The Illegitimate Duchess

Historical Essay

Written by Shelley R. Riley
Researched by Stephen A. Riley

Published by Leeatra Studio

Registered in New York

www.leeatra.com

ISBN 978-1-935734-50-5

Cover image: By Konstantin Andreyevich Ukhtomsky - A.H. Voronihina, Halls of the Hermitage and Winter Palace, watercolors, in the mid-20th century, Moscow Art 1983. Original untouched image: Image: Nicholas Hall.jpg 1866, Public Domain, https://commons. wikimedia.org/w/index.php?curid= 5244575. **The Winter Palace was the birthplace of Anna Petrovna, the second child of Catherine the Great.**

Definition : **Russian Duchess** : "A title given to daughters and male-line grand-daughters of the Emperors or Empress Regnants of Russia, as well as to wives of Grand Dukes of Russia" *('List of Grand Duchesses of Russia').*

It is hoped that our years of genealogical research will make the case and set the framework for proving that our ancestor Ann Elizabeth de Daschkopf is actually Grand Duchess Anna Petrovna* of Russia, the illegitimate daughter of Empress Catherine the Great.

* There were two people from Russia named Anna Petrovna. Our story is about the second Anna Petrovna, who was named after the first Anna Petrovna, sister of Empress Elizabeth.

Table of Contents

I.

Introduction

My husband, Stephen Riley, knew his ancestors were from Ireland, Germany, France and Canada, but the idea of having an ancestor from Russia was unexpected and incredibly intriguing. The document that started it all—and gave him the very first clue—was a record from the Church of the Latter-day Saints "International Genealogical Index" (IGI) of his fourth great grandmother:

Ann or Elizabeth de Daschkopf
Gender: female
Birth: about 1759...of Russia
Death: 14 March 1857
        Loretto, Cambria, Pa.,USA
Burial: March 1857
        Loretto Cem.,Cambria,Pa., USA
Marriage (1):
Spouse: John Wharton
Marriage: about 1786
        Philadelphia, Philadelphia, Penna., USA

Eighteenth century records are sparse to non-existent in most cases but we were able to trace Ann Elizabeth de Daschkopf's life from the time she married in America (when she was in her late twenties) up to her death about 70 years later. Gravestones, government documents, church records, and other written accounts have come together to create a picture of her life in this country. De Daschkopf was alive on this earth for 98 years! This information was fascinating, but we wanted to learn more about her "missing years," those years from her birth in Russia until her arrival in America. This led us on an intriguing quest

Online genealogical record of Ann
Elizabeth de Daschkopf.

where we discovered the information you'll read in this book.

We were curious—could a child of Russian (possibly royal) ancestry really end up in a small Catholic wilderness community in western Pennsylvania? And if so, how?

This book will give the known facts as well as our suppositions as we believe they may have occurred. It requires a leap of faith to examine the facts and then to weave all of the coincidences of de Daschkopf's story to the famous and unknown connections who gave her a start in life.

II.

Main Character Bios

Ann Elizabeth de Daschkopf's story involves a number of characters, including some rather exciting ones…

Ann Elizabeth de Daschkopf

Stanislaus Warthon / Wharton

Father Demetrius Augustine Gallitzin

Catherine The Great

Stanislaus Augustus Poniatowski

ANN ELIZABETH de DASCHKOPF / ANN WARTHON

ANN ELIZABETH de DASCHKOPF was born in December 1758 "about 1759" in Russia. She married John (or Joseph*) Warthon in Philadelphia about 1786. De Daschkopf was nearly 30 when she married Warthon, and one wonders if this was her first marriage, since women of the time generally married at a much younger age. We do not have a copy of her actual marriage certificate.

The years between her birth and her marriage remain a mystery. After her marriage we know a bit more. De Daschkopf and Warthon had seven children all born between the years of 1788 and 1802 in Maryland, somewhere about 40 miles from Baltimore. Sometime between 1802 and 1809 her husband died, probably in Maryland. By 1810, de Daschkopf and her seven children had traveled across the Alleghenies to western Pennsylvania to Loretto, a community founded in 1799 by the Catholic missionary priest Father Demetrius Augustine Gallitzin (Gallitzin, "Pascal Con."). She and her family lived in close proximity to each other and to Gallitzin from 1810 through the rest of their lives. De Daschkopf and some of her daughters worked for Gallitzin, and were closely connected to him. De Daschkopf died at age 98 in Loretto, Cambria County, Pennsylvania, on March 14, 1857. She is buried in the Loretto Church of St. Michael's Cemetery nearby her beloved priest (St. Michael's Church records).

*JOSEPH WARTHON: In the St. Michael's Church records in Loretto, PA of the marriages of de Daschkopf's children, their father is listed as Joseph. Some accounts say he was English but we believe he was German.

SPELLING ODDITIES AND INCONSISTENCIES

Ann or Elizabeth de Daschkopf:
Although her name is listed as Ann OR Elizabeth, for the purposes of this book we will list her as Ann Elizabeth. The name Daschkopf is a German variation of the Russian Dashkov (male) and Dashkova (female). De Daschkopf's use of the German spelling may have been used to throw off the suggestion of a Russian birth.

Catherine Warthon, Widow Warthon:
In "The Memorandum Book and the Account Book of Rev. Demetrius A. Gallitzin," the editor Escalante mentions Gallitzin's use of these names—Catherine Warthon, Widow Warthon—for de Daschkopf, concluding that the Widow Warthon's "Christian name seems to have been Catherine" (29, 54, 56).

Ann Warthon, Widow:
In Gallizin's lists of Easter communicants and confessions he referred to de Daschkopf as Ann Warthon, Widow, instead of as Catherine (Gallitzin, "Pascal Con."). Gallitzin wasn't consistent.

De Daschkopf's married name:
Warthon: This is the original spelling.
Wharton: Sometime during her son Stanislaus' lifetime he changed the spelling of his last name to Wharton (see comparisons of various federal census records).
Wathin: This is used on her gravestone.

The tombstone of Ann Wathin/Ann Elizabeth de Daschkopf Warthon found in St. Michael's Cemetery in Loretto, Cambria County, PA.
Albert Ledoux http://findagrave.com/cgi-bin/fg.cgi? page= pv&GRid=86335123

WARTHON FAMILY REFERENCE

Ann Warthon could refer to mother or daughter
Ann Wathin is the spelling on de Daschkopf's tombstone
Catherine Warthon/Wharton could be:

- Daughter of Ann Elizabeth de Daschkopf and Joseph Warthon (1790-1854)
- Ann Elizabeth de Daschkopf Warthon, whose Christian name was Catherine (about 1758-1857)

STANISLAUS WARTHON / WHARTON

It is important to include information in this book about de Daschkopf's only son, STANISLAUS WARTHON/WHARTON, since much of what we were able to discover about de Daschkopf was through his records. (Male records are much more specific than female records during our country's earliest years.) These records include U.S. census records (see Chapter V for more details) and the Cambria, Co., PA archives. He was born somewhere between 1791 and 1793 in Maryland and arrived in Loretto, PA by 1810. In the summer of 1812, he served as a private with the 2nd Regiment Riflemen (the Pipers) during the War of 1812. He married Mary McConnell, in St. Augustine, PA in 1813, and served as county commissioner in 1825. After his mother (de Daschkopf) died, he retired from farming and moved his family to nearby St. Augustine, PA to open a grocery store in 1861. He also served as postmaster of St. Augustine. He died there on January 26, 1873 and is buried in the Catholic Church Cemetery of St. Augustine.

The tombstone of Stanislaus Wharton and his wife Mary McConnell found in St. Augustine Cemetery in St. Augustine, Cambria County, PA.
Photo by Shelley R. Riley, 2003

FATHER DEMETRIUS AUGUSTINE GALLITZIN

DEMETRIUS AUGUSTINE GALLITZIN was born in The
Hague, Netherlands on December 22, 1770. His father was
Prince Dmitrii Golitsyn of Russia, Russian ambassador to
France and later the Netherlands. At the request of Catherine
the Great, Prince Golitsyn helped secure the purchase of French
philosopher and writer Diderot's 3000 book library for Russia
(Troyat 202, 203) (Cronin 228), and also helped in the purchase
of paintings for her private collection, which eventually became
the Hermitage Museum (Troyat 215). Demetrius Gallitzin's
mother was a Prussian countess, the daughter of Field Marshall
Schmettau. He had a sister, Marian/Mimi, who was one year
older. In about 1772, Catherine the Great toured Europe to
avoid the plague spreading throughout Russia. She was present
for Gallitzin's baptism into the Russian Orthodox Church, and
served as his godmother ("Cause for..." part 1). She held him
in her arms and appointed him an officer of the guard (Brownson 16). The young Gallitzin, his sister, and mother traveled

to Germany many times. He was also given military training and studied engineering, preparing to be a professional soldier. But in 1787, when he and his mother and sister converted to Catholicism, all that changed ("Dem. A. Gallitzin").

As an aristocratic young man of that time, he was expected to continue his education by going on a "grand tour" of Europe. However, with much of Europe at war, he was sent to America in 1792, under the care of a young priest tutor. Traveling under the name of Augustine Schmettau, and later Augustine Smith, he arrived in Baltimore, at the residence of Bishop John Carroll, with letters of introduction from European prince-priests. Eventually he studied for the priesthood, giving up all his royal rights, privileges, and inheritance. In spite of this, he repeatedly sent to Europe asking for his due inheritance, which he wanted to use for his mission work. He received little of it ("Dem. A. Gallitzin").

Gallitzin was ordained Father Augustine Smith in 1795. He traveled very humbly to work at missions in Maryland, Virginia, West Virginia, and Pennsylvania, and eventually founded the first English speaking mission in the Alleghenies, in Loretto, Cambria County, PA, in 1799. He used his engineering skills to lay out the new town. In 1802, Father Smith became a naturalized citizen but it wasn't until 1809 that he petitioned to be officially known, once again, as Demetrius Augustine Gallitzin. He died May 6, 1840 in Loretto, PA and is buried there. In 2005, Gallitzin was named a Servant of God by the Congregation for the Causes of Saints, the first step toward possible future sainthood ("Cause for..." part 1-13).

A stained glass depiction of Father Demetrius Gallitzin and Father Peter Helbron, early Catholic missionaries in Western Pennsylvania. The window is located in St Patrick's Roman Catholic Church in Canonsburg, PA.

GOLITSYN FAMILY

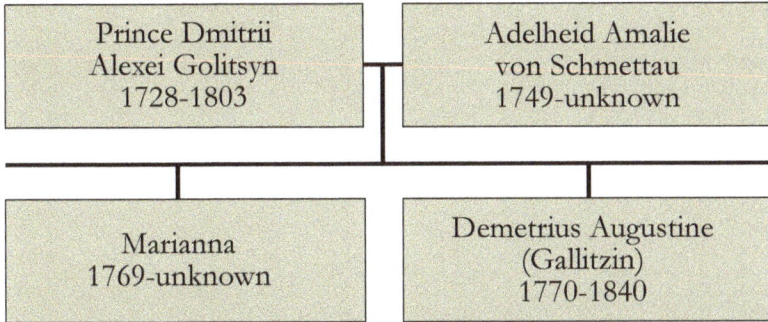

Prince Dmitrii Alexei Golitsyn 1728-1803	Adelheid Amalie von Schmettau 1749-unknown

Marianna 1769-unknown	Demetrius Augustine (Gallitzin) 1770-1840

In historical records, Father Gallitzin is sometimes referred to as Augustine Schmettau or Augustine Smith.

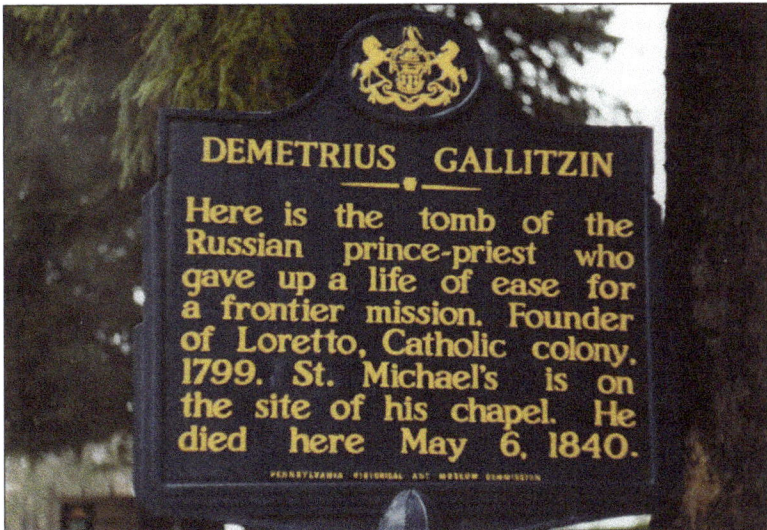

Historical marker for Demetrius Gallitzin in Pennsylvania.
By Eric W. Miller www.antiquesshowpromotions.com - Own work, CC BY 3.0, https://commons.wikimedia.org/w/index.php?curid=15066768

CATHERINE THE GREAT

CATHERINE THE GREAT (Catherine II) was born on May 2, 1729 in Stettin, Pomerania, Prussia (now Szczecin, Poland). Her birth name was SOPHIA AUGUSTA FREDERICKA von ANHALT-ZERBST-DORNBURG, and her father was a German Lutheran aristocrat. The Empress Elizabeth (Petrovna), daughter of Peter the Great and Catherine I, was on the Russian throne with no children of her own when she chose her late sister Anna's son, Peter III, to become heir to the throne upon her death. She chose Sophia to be Peter's wife. Both were very young at the time. Peter and Sophia were both German by birth, although Peter was part Russian. Sophia immersed herself into her new country, learned how to speak Russian, switched from the Lutheran religion of her childhood to join the Russian Orthodox Church, and embraced Russian culture (Troyat 29). Sophia was received into the church in 1744 and given the name CATHERINE (Troyat 35, 36).

The following year, at age 16, Catherine married Peter III, but the marriage was never happy. While Catherine tried to be as Russian as she could be, her husband loved Prussian culture. During this time, Catherine became friends with Ekaterina Vorontsova-Dashkova. They both shared a love of intellectual conversation about a wide range of topics. After Empress Elizabeth died, Peter III ruled Russia briefly until a coup, partly led by Catherine's friend, Dashkova, overthrew him and placed Catherine on the throne (Dashkova 65-93). During Catherine's long reign (1762-1796), Russia modernized, grew stronger, and became a European power. Catherine was a patron of the arts and the Hermitage Museum began as her personal art collection. She ruled until her death in 1796, at the age of 67, in St. Petersburg ("Cath. the Great").

An aerial view of the Winter Palace, Hermitage Museum in Saint Petersburg, Russia. Catherine the Great founded the Hermitage Museum in 1764.

By Andrew Shiva / Wikipedia, CC BY-SA 4.0, https://commons.wikimedia.org/w/index. php?curid=51992181

Oil on canvas portrait of Empress Catherine the Great.
By Fyodor Rokotov - http://www.art-catalog.ru/index.php, Public Domain, https://commons.wikimedia.org/w/index.php?curid=5110929

Russian monarchs and their years on the throne:

- Tsar Peter I (Peter the Great): 1682-1725
- Empress Catherine I (wife of Peter the Great): 1725-1727
- Tsar Peter II (a grandson of Peter the Great): 1727-1730
- Empress Anna Ivanovna (niece of Peter the Great, cousin of Empress Elizabeth): 1730-1740
- Tsar Ivan VI: (1740-1741)
- Empress Elizabeth (daughter of Peter the Great): 1741 -1761
- Tsar Peter III (a grandson of Peter the Great, husband of Catherine the Great): 1761-1762
- Empress Catherine II (Catherine the Great): 1762-1796
- Tsar Paul I (son of Catherine the Great, widely believed to be the son of Serge Saltykov, not Peter III): 1796-1801

RUSSIAN IMPERIAL FAMILY

(Connected to our story, with birth and death dates)

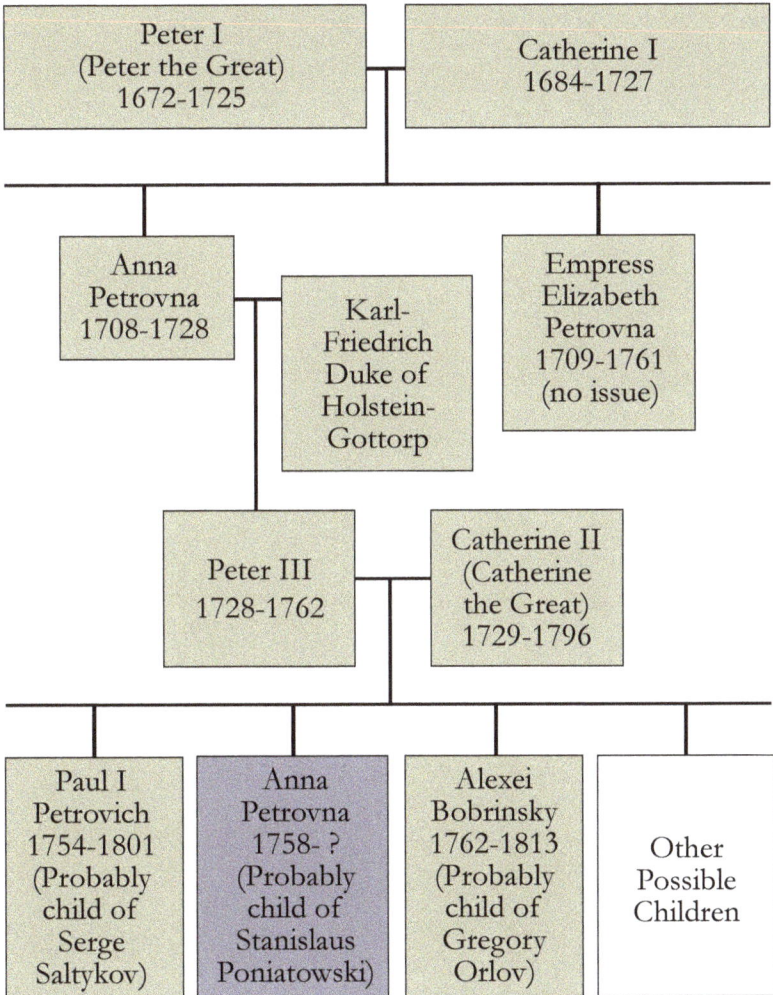

Peter I (Peter the Great) 1672-1725	Catherine I 1684-1727

Anna Petrovna 1708-1728	Karl-Friedrich Duke of Holstein-Gottorp	Empress Elizabeth Petrovna 1709-1761 (no issue)

Peter III 1728-1762	Catherine II (Catherine the Great) 1729-1796

Paul I Petrovich 1754-1801 (Probably child of Serge Saltykov)	Anna Petrovna 1758- ? (Probably child of Stanislaus Poniatowski)	Alexei Bobrinsky 1762-1813 (Probably child of Gregory Orlov)	Other Possible Children

The use of the name Petrovna refers to "daughter of Peter."

STANISLAUS AUGUSTUS PONIATOWSKI

STANISLAUS AUGUSTUS PONIATOWSKI was born on January 17, 1732 in Wolczyn, in the Polish Lithuanian Common-wealth in what is now Belarus. His family was Polish nobility, giving him the title of Grand Duke of Lithuania. During his life he traveled a lot and lived in many places including Gdansk and Warsaw, Poland; Paris, France; Germany and the Netherlands. In 1755, he came to St. Petersburg at the request of the British ambassador to Russia, Sir Charles Hanbury-Williams, who was hoping to create an alliance against France ("S.A. Poniatowski"). There, Poniatowski met Catherine the Great, three years his senior, and fell madly in love with her (Cronin 106). Perhaps hoping to bolster his career, he left Russia in 1756, but returned in 1757. He was presumed to be the father of Catherine's second child, Anna Petrovna, who was born in December of 1758. By April 1759, he was expelled from Russia by Empress Elizabeth, not for his politics or his nationality, but because he was Catholic (Cronin 120).

In 1764, he was set up by the Russian government to become the next King of Poland, since Russia hoped for a strong alliance with that country. He attempted to strengthen and reform the country while other countries, including Russia, wanted it to be kept weak (Cronin 186). He was a patron of the arts, establishing a national theater, and he supported growth in astronomy, edu-cation, literature, and the sciences, cartography and industry. His reign was ruined by constant interference from Russia and the partitions of his country in 1772, 1793 and 1795. Poniatowski, the "last King of Poland," abdicated in 1795, and spent his re-maining years in semi-captivity in St Petersburg. He died there, of a stroke, February 12, 1798 and is now buried in Warsaw, in the St. John's Archcathedral ("S.A. Poniatowski").

Election of Stanislaus Augustus Poniatowski, 1764.

By Bernardo Bellotto - Lileyko Jerzy (1980). Vademecum Zamku Warszawskiego, Warszawa. ISBN 83-22318-18-9, Public Domain, https://commons.wikimedia.org/w/index.php?curid=2777946

Portrait of Stanislaus Augustus Poniatowski in coronation robes.
By Marcello Bacciarelli - Own work (BurgererSF), Public Domain, https://commons.wikimedia.org/w/index.php?curid=2778013

III.

Minor Character Bios

The following two people are possible minor characters in our story, but they are not minor characters in history.

Ekaterina Vorontsova-Dashkova

Empress Elizabeth Petrovna

EKATERINA VORONTSOVA-DASHKOVA, a COUNTESS

EKATERINA VORONTSOVA-DASHKOVA, a COUNTESS, was born on March 28, 1743 in St. Petersburg, Russia into an aristocratic family who served its country's government. Her father was Count Vorontsov, a member of the Russian Senate, and her brother was Russian ambassador to Great Britain (Dashkova 333). At a young age, she went to live with her uncle, an educated man with a huge library (Woronzoff-Dashkoff 12-14, 17, 22). She received an excellent education, and studied math at the University of Moscow. She was extremely well read and became friends with Diderot and Voltaire, both philosophers and writers, with whom she met personally over the years. By the age of 15, she had met and become friends with 30 year old Catherine, the future Catherine the Great, who was then a German princess married to Peter III, heir to the Russian throne ("Y.V. Dashkova").

Before she was 16, Ekaterina married Prince Mikhail Dashkov (1736-1764), who was from a prominent Russian noble family who lived in Moscow. There she learned to speak Russian, having grown up speaking French ("Y.V. Dashkova").

In 1761, when Empress Elizabeth died, Peter III became ruler and Catherine became Empress Consort. A few months later, Peter was overthrown, abdicated, and died. According to her own memoirs, Ekaterina played a leading part in this coup d'etat that put Catherine the Great on the throne (Dashkova 76-86), although Catherine the Great downplayed this in her own memoirs ("Y.V. Dashkova").

Catherine appointed Dashkova's husband to be the Russian Field Marshall who would lead a coup that would place Stanislaus Poniatowski on the Polish throne. Mikhail Dashkov died in Poland in 1764 (Woronzoff-Dashkoff 109-112).

After that, Dashkova's relationship with Catherine was on-again and off-again over many years. At times they were close confidants yet at other times there was hostility between them (Woronzoff-Dashkoff 49-70). During times when she was out of favor, Dashkova made two European trips, the first from 1769-1771, the second from 1775-1782. She stayed with prominent people and personal friends, met heads of state from many countries, intellectuals in math and literature and made useful political and intellectual connections (97-149).

On her return, and again in favor, Catherine appointed Dashkova as head of what is today known as the Russian Academy of Sciences. Dashkova also began work on a six-volume Russian dictionary. Benjamin Franklin appointed her the first female member of the American Philosophical Society in Philadelphia, and he became the first American member of the Russian Academy of Sciences (Amer. Phil. Soc. exhibit notes). Dashkova died on her Moscow estate on January 4, 1810 ("Y.V. Dashkova").

VORONTSOVA-DASHKOVA FAMILY

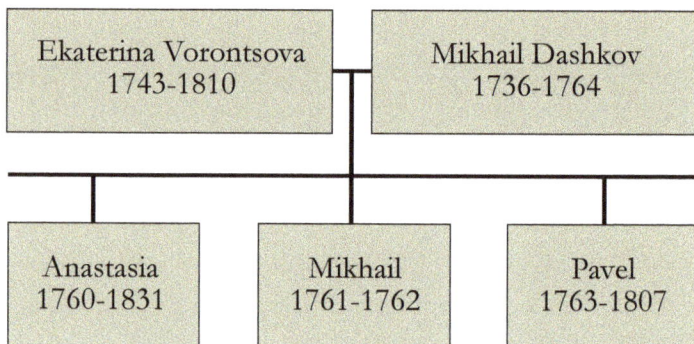

Ekaterina Vorontsova 1743-1810	Mikhail Dashkov 1736-1764

Anastasia 1760-1831	Mikhail 1761-1762	Pavel 1763-1807

Portrait of the Princess Yekaterina R. Vorontsova-Dashkova (1743-1810), the first President of the Russian Academy of Sciences. Museum of Architecture and Art, Alupka.

By Levitsky, Dmitri Grigorievich (1735-1822) - fine-art-images.net/en/showIMG_15244.html, Public Domain, https://commons.wikimedia.org/w/index.php?curid=28209569

EMPRESS ELIZABETH PETROVNA

EMPRESS ELIZABETH PETROVNA, daughter of Peter the Great, never married and had no children and therefore no heirs, so she chose her nephew, Peter III, son of her late sister, Anna, to succeed her to the Russian throne. She chose Sophia, the future Catherine the Great, to be his wife ("Eliz. of Russia").

Catherine's mother was cousin to Empress Elizabeth's fiancé, before their planned marriage and his early death ("Eliz. of Russia").

Empress Elizabeth, and her nephew, Peter III, were godparents to Ekaterina Vorontsova (Dashkova) (Woronzoff-Dashkoff 5). Empress Elizabeth was also godmother to Anna Petrovna, Catherine the Great's second child ("Cath. the Great").

Empress Elizabeth spoke French, German and Italian. She was vain and extravagant, not particularly intelligent, but helped modernize Russia and was a popular ruler. She built the Winter Palace ("Eliz. of Russia").

Portrait of Empress Elizabeth Petrovna. Unknown artist. 18th century. Ministry of Culture of the Russian Federation, via Google Cultural Institute.

By Unknown - Google Art Project, Public Domain, https://commons.wikimedia.org/w/index. php?curid=40095259

IV.

Facts:

Who
Ann Elizabeth de Daschkopf
Was <u>Not</u>

Various family genealogists have suggested theories of Ann Elizabeth de Daschkopf's ancestry which we have found are incorrect:

1. Some say Andrei Iakovlevich Dashkov was her father. He was born in St. Petersburg, Russia in 1775 and was appointed by Czar Aleksandr I as Chargé d'Affaires, and Consul General to the US. While living in Philadelphia, PA, from 1809 until 1817, Andrei Iakovlevich Dashkov served as Russian ambassador to the new United States of America, during the presidencies of Madison and Monroe. He was fluent in Russian, French, German and English and could read German and Latin. He died in 1831 ("A.Y. Daskov"). In his diplomatic duties, he was involved with trying to help Gallitzin obtain funds from his family in Russia (The United States and Russia 625, 1084, 1085), but… he can't be de Daschkopf's father, since he was born about 18 years after she was!

2. We found that a lot more has been recorded and written about de Daschkopf's son, Stanislaus, than was written about her. The following account appears in a 1908 historical publication about the people who settled in the Pittsburgh area: "Stanislaus Wharton's mother was Ann Knopp and is said to have been the daughter of a prime minister of England to Poland" (Boucher 43, vol. 4). That sounded intriguing although technically there is no "prime minister of England to Poland" and so it presented more questions than answers. This also seems to be the only reference to her last name of Knopp, although it could be a shortening of the name de Daschkopf. We believe this is perhaps a hint that her birth father was indeed the King (Prime

Minister) of Poland, Stanislaus Poniatowski. As the future King of Poland, Poniatowski did have British connections. He met with the British ambassador to Russia first in Berlin, and then traveled to England in 1754, where he met with the future Lord Chancellor of Great Britain. He came to Russia in 1755 ("S. A. Poniatowski").

3. There was initial thought that de Daschkopf was related to Ekaterina Vorontsova-Dashkova (1743-1810). Dashkova was closely linked to the life of Catherine the Great (1729-1796) from about the age of 15. Ekaterina married Mikhail Dashkov (1736-1764) a prominent Russian nobleman, about 1759, the same year de Daschkopf was born, but their three known children were Pavel (a Russian engineer), Anastasia and Mikhail, who died young (Dashkova 27). However, we do believe there could be some connection to de Daschkopf and the use of the name Dashkova/Dashkov. (See Chapter VIII "Our Theories: The Missing Years" for more details about this.) Secondly, the only way that Mikhail Dashkov could be Anna Petrovna's father is if he had an affair with Catherine the Great shortly before the arrival of Poniatowski. None of the biographies of Catherine even hint of this. Lastly, another way to prove/disprove if Mikhail Dashkov was involved is to consider the DNA of Stephen Riley, the researcher of this book. If Mikhail Dashkov were an ancestor, Riley's DNA would have to include a Russian link. We are fairly certain it does not.

V.

Facts:

How Ann Elizabeth de Daschkopf Was Connected to Father Demetrius Gallitzin

The following is a chronological time-line of Ann Elizabeth de Daschkopf and her family's life as they settled into Loretto, Cambria County, PA, intertwined with events in Father Demetrius Gallitzin's life during the same time. *Information in this section comes from various records in the public domain including ancestry.com, the Church of Latter-day Saints website www.familysearch.org as well as records from Cambria Co., PA archives, St. Michael's Church and the gravesites of St. Michael's Cemetery in Loretto, Cambria County, PA.*

In 1786, Gallitzin's mother returned to Catholicism after following the Russian Orthodox religion, the religion of the Russian aristocracy. By 1787, Gallitzin became Catholic, too. He chose Augustine as his confirmation name, for the Feast of St. Augustine on August 28, the date of his mother's birth and marriage ("Dem. A. Gallitzin").

About 1786, de Daschkopf married Joseph Warthon, probably in Philadelphia.

About 1788, de Daschkopf gave birth to her first daughter, Theresa, in Maryland.

About 1790, de Daschkopf gave birth to her second daughter, Catherine, in Maryland.

About 1792/93, de Daschkopf gave birth to her first and only son, Stanislaus, in Maryland.

The actual town, or towns, in Maryland where her children were born is unknown, although it is suggested that Stanislaus was born "40 miles from Baltimore," so Frederick, MD or Howard, Columbia County, MD are possibilities. Some of his birth records say he was born in Washington, DC. The DC area split off from Maryland in 1792, about the time Stanislaus was born, so this could put his birth in Montgomery or Prince George Counties in Maryland. His six sisters were probably born in the same place.

In 1792, young Prince Gallitzin arrived in Baltimore incognito under the name Augustine Schmettau, later Schmet or Smith. He was known as Augustine Smith for many years. He met directly with Bishop Carroll, who directed his studies and guided his education. Six weeks after his arrival, Carroll wrote to Gallitzin's mother from Baltimore. He referred to her son as "Monsr. Schmidt" and asked her about financial arrangements for him. He also told her that her son would be doing missionary work and visiting the sick in outposts of the diocese (The United States and Russia, Letter #42, 285-286.).

By the end of 1792, Gallitzin had begun studying for the priesthood in St. Sulpice Seminary in Baltimore. His studies included mission trips to neighboring states and towns ("Dem. A. Gallitzin").

Following his spring 1795 ordination by Bishop Carroll, Gallitzin was given a vacation in Georgetown, 40 miles west of Baltimore. On the way back he took a 150 mile circuit into southern Maryland, hoping to see more of the rural areas of the country. He spent a long time in Port Tobacco, Charles County—the most concentrated Catholic area in the U.S.—where he wished to spend the rest of his life. He was, however, called back to Baltimore and sent on to Conewago, PA in August of 1795 ("Cause for..." part 8). His new missionary work was as a "circuit rider" missionary priest. His circuit covered territory in Maryland and Virginia, as well as southeast counties in Pennsylvania and as far west as Huntingdon, PA in all directions for 150 miles. He hoped to visit each community once a month this way ("Cause for..." part 9).

About 1796, de Daschkopf gave birth to her third daughter, Mary, in Maryland.

About 1797, de Daschkopf gave birth to her fourth daughter, Ann, in Maryland

About 1799, de Daschkopf gave birth to her fifth daughter Ellen/Eleanor, in Maryland.

Gallitzin loved his missionary work, and knew there was a need for him in western Pennsylvania. He was ready to start missionary work on his own. In 1799, Gallitzin left Baltimore, "in a two-horse prairie schooner, in which were stored an altar, sacred vessels, altar wine, flour, coffee, a bed, a bureau and more than 100 books" ("Cause for..." part 9).

In 1799, Gallitzin founded the town of Loretto, PA using his engineering skills to lay out the town on a gentle hillside slope. In a letter to Bishop Carroll he wrote, "Our church is about 44 feet long by 25 feet, built of white pine logs with a very good shingle roof…There is also a house built for me, 16 feet by 14, besides a little kitchen and a stable….The congregation numbers at present about 40 families" ("Cause for..." part 9). It was the first English-speaking Catholic settlement in the United States west of the Allegheny Front. He dedicated the parish church to St. Michael, the Archangel, honoring his Russian roots. In Russia, nearly every large city has a church or chapel dedicated to Archangel Michael. Many monasteries and cathedrals have that name as well.

Gallitzin named his town Loretto, after the famous Italian shrine. Each evening he, and any household members, liked to recite a litany about Loretto, and to say the rosary ("Cause for..." part 9).

In the 1800 U.S. census, Gallitzin was listed as "Augustine Smith" in the Huntingdon, Allegheny County, PA census, with a household of seven (probably orphans he cared for). Loretto was originally part of Huntingdon County, but once Cambria County was formed, Loretto was a village within Allegheny Township, in the county of Cambria, PA.

In 1802, Gallitzin became a naturalized U.S. citizen.

About 1802, de Daschkopf gave birth to her sixth daughter, Martha, in Maryland.

In 1809, Gallitzin petitioned to become officially known once again as Demetrius Augustine Gallitzin, a return to his birth name.

Somewhere between 1802 and 1809, we assume de Daschkopf's husband, Joseph Warthon, died, probably in Maryland, and the family decided to head west. Lacking any exact information on this it's hard to pinpoint his death date with more exactness, but the last child was born in 1802 and Loretto records from 1810 on refer to her as a widow (Widow Ann).

It's interesting to note that it was also in 1809 that Father Augustine Smith changed his name back to Father Demetrius Gallitzin.

At about this same time, the Warthon family (de Daschkopf and her children ranging in age from seven or eight up to their early 20s) moved north westward across the wilderness of the Allegheny Mountains with other hardy pioneers, to settle in Cambria County, Pennsylvania.

The trip from Maryland to Loretto was difficult, along unpaved rocky, muddy and root covered roads. One wonders if the Warthons journeyed by foot, wagon or horseback. However they went, they were true pioneers. A description of various Catholic trails leading west from the more settled eastern shore explains that "most of these trails" could be "traced to wild animals searching for food or drink long before the appearance of man. The Indians adopted them, because they led to water and salt licks and followed the lines of least resistance. The white man, in turn, adopted the Indian trails, at first on foot or horseback and later widened for wagons. Paths of least resistance were particularly required in a land of mountain ranges, running on the diagonal" (Cath. Trails West iii).

We do not know where the Warthons lived in Maryland and so do not know the particular trails they would have traveled to the Loretto mission.

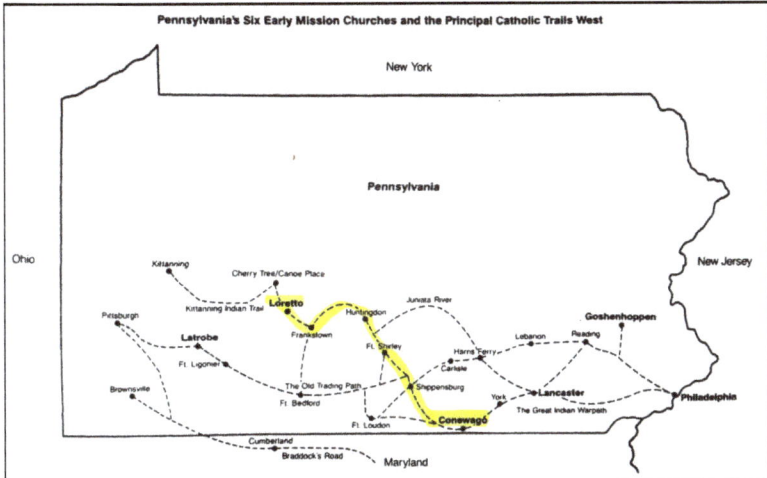

Pennsylvania's Six Early Mission Churches and the Principal Catholic Trails West

This map shows the locations of the early Pennsylvania mission churches and the main trails to them. Most settlers began in the Baltimore and Philadelphia areas, where there was quite of bit of religious intolerance toward Catholics, and followed a combination of trails into the sparsely settled areas to the west. Those from eastern Maryland headed northwest across the state and north to Conewago, PA (Cath. Trails West vol. 1, ii, iii, vii).

The following is from the list of "Pascal Confessions and Communions and Confirmations of Loretto, Cambria County, PA from 1810-1813." (Gallitzin, "Pascal Con."). It places de Daschkopf ("The Widow Ann Warthon, whom Gallitzin often refers to as Catherine") in Loretto by 1810:

Pascal Communions for 1810:
Catherine McConnell, wife *(probably wife of Arthur McConnell)*
Ann Warthon, single *(daughter of Ann)*
Ann Warthon, widow *(Ann Elizabeth de Daschkopf Warthon)*
Catherine Warthon, single *(daughter of Ann)*

Mary McConnell, single *(daughter of Arthur, Stanislaus' future wife)*
Susan McConnell, single
Margaret McConnell, single
Mary Warthon, single *(daughter of Ann)*
Sarah McConnell, single
Theresa Warthon, single *(daughter of Ann)*
Mary McConnell, wife
Margaret McConnell, wife
Daniel McConnell
John McConnell, Sr.

In a similar 1811 list, many of the same names appeared, including the name Ann Warthon twice. We presume this referred to mother and daughter.

In 1813, Ann Warthon's name appeared again.

In the 1810 U.S. census, records showed that "Stana Wurthen" was among a group of settlers in Allegheny Township, Cambria County and the head of a household of six. On the line below him is listed "Smith Galatzon DD" (Father Demetrius Gallitzin), heading a household of seven. As early as 1805, Gallitzin had begun to care for orphans in his community, the first ones being the McConnell children, cousins of Stanislaus' future wife.

An explanation of the inexactness of early U.S. census records: The U.S. census was, and is, taken every 10 years. The first U.S. census was in 1790, and was rather imprecise, as were so many from the following decades. In the 1810 census record "Stana Warthen's" household consisted of one free white male between

16 and 25 (probably refers to himself), one white female under 10 (probably Martha), two free white females between 10 and 15 (probably Ellen or Ann or Mary), one 16-25 (either Catherine or Theresa) and one 26 to 44 (too young for his mother de Daschkopf). If that is not de Daschkopf, and we do know she was there in Loretto, with whom was she listed? More details were added to the census records as time went on, such as the exact names and ages of all household members, their relationship to the head of the household, their occupations, their places of birth and so on.

In summer 1812, Stanislaus Warthon fought in the War of 1812, as a member of the 2nd Regiment Riflemen (Pipers) of Pennsylvania, and from his pension application we learn he served under Captain Richard McGuire of the Pennsylvania militia. The McGuires were very early settlers to the Cambria County area. The Pennsylvania Department of Military Affairs lists Stanislaus as being in the 142nd Regt. Inf. 1st Brig, 12th Div, with the rank of Private.

In 1813, after returning from the war, Stanislaus married Mary McConnell. She was born in Emmittsburg, MD about 1792, the daughter of Arthur McConnell and Catherine Moury, both born in County Antrim, Northern Ireland. She and her parents had arrived in the Loretto community in 1807. Arthur's brother and his wife and family were also there. Mary McConnell Warthon was a deeply religious woman who worked for Gallitzin for many years (Mary Wharton obit). Stanislaus and his family were considered pioneer settlers of Loretto who cleared and cultivated a large tract of land.

Quite a few books have been written about Gallitzin and the community of Loretto. One item which gives an interesting account of the day-to-day functioning of the community and its members is "The Memorandum Book and Account Book" of Demetrius Gallitzin, containing entries from about 1804-1824. It is "part register, part a journal, and still another part a house book"(5). The original book is in poor and disordered condition. Five pages have been removed (6) and one can't help wondering why. Perhaps they contained information someone wanted concealed and were removed on purpose?

The editor, Escalante, analyzed the varied entries and determined that the community was run mainly by barter and exchanges of goods, even though as one reads through it, it seems as though Gallitzin had time to farm as well as minister to his flock. But just as he was paid in goods and services rather than in actual currency, so he paid out his bills and debts to others (Gallitzin, Mem. Book, 61-63).

The following excerpts are of particular interest to us since they place de Daschkopf/the Widow Ann, also sometimes referred to by Gallitzin as Catherine, and her children within the community of Loretto and within the company of Gallitzin. Gallitzin opened accounts for various named persons, one of whom is "Catherine Warthon, elsewhere referred to as 'Widow Warthon', for various sundries" (Gallitzin, The Mem. Book 29).

Gallitzin dealt in grain and flour and in an entry titled "1814 flour lent and sold" are names of the buyers and borrowers, one of the purchasers being "Widow Warthon" (Gallitzin, The Mem. Book 54).

THE WIDOW WARTHON'S ACCOUNTS. The entries relating to a certain Widow Warthon, whose Christian name seems to have been Catherine, and a spinner and weaver by occupation, take up several pages in the book, namely, the whole of page 43, 62 and 63, and nearly the whole of pages 68, 72 and 73. I* select a few of the entries, namely: on September 2, apparently in the year 1814, she is credited with weaving 36 yards at 10 cents a yard; on December 22, 30 yards at the same price; again with "spinning 5 weeks, $3.45;" on March 31, with weaving "30 yards Tow at 8 cents" and "31 yards of Cotton" at 12 cents a yard. For November 1, I find this entry, viz: "the girls worked 5 days at 40 cents" a day.

Further on the widow is credited with "5 days Work in harvest at 40 cents, $2.00; "then, "20 ½ doz. Wollen Yarn" spun at 25 cts., $5.12 ½; "5 ¾ Doz. flax at 25 cts., $1.44"; 17½ Linnen [sic] wove at 10 cents, $1.95". After May 8, apparently in 1814, she spins "Wool 14 Doz and 9 Cutts at 15 cts. a Day, $2.47", after the same month in 1816, "28 yards Shirting at 12½ cents, $3.50", and "23 yards of Linsey at [the same price], $2.88', while in July, she spins "15 Doz[en and] 9 Cutts 25 cts., $3.92."

*Refers to the editor Escalante. Entire excerpt taken from *The Memorandum Book and The Account Book of Rev. Demetrius A. Gallitzin*, page 56.

One can assume that de Daschkopf was living in close proximity to her son and his family, and some of her daughters, as we read through the following decades of census records for Stanislaus Warthon (again which give only the barest of information on each of the other household members).

In the 1820 U.S. census from Allegheny, Cambria County, PA. Stanislaus's name was spelled Stanislaus Warthan. Six people were in this household. He was married by then.

On August 31, 1824, de Daschkopf's youngest daughter, Martha, married John (Johannes) Ivory.

In the 1830 U.S. census of Cambria County, PA. Stanislaus's name was spelled Wharton. There were 11 people in his household.

On May 6, 1840, Father Demetrius Augustine Gallitzin died, in Loretto, PA, sick and weak after years of traveling in the wilderness to visit his parishioners. He had used his own money to help build his parish and never saw most of what was to have been his inheritance from Russia. He is buried in St. Michael's Cemetery, Loretto, Cambria County, PA ("Dem. A. Gallitzin").

In his will, Gallitzin gave all the buildings and lands to various bishops for the continuation of the church. Money was also given to the Wharton family: "I give and bequeath to Mary Wharton [think this refers to the Mary Wharton who was Stanislaus' wife, not the Mary who was Ann's daughter] the sum of five hundred dollars to be paid by my Executor to her. I give and bequeath to Catherine Wharton [this probably refers to Ann de Daschkopf, since Gallitzin elsewhere calls the widow Ann by "her Christian name, Catherine"] the sum of <u>two hundred and seventy five dollars</u> [the words "two hundred and seventy five" were underlined in the original document and would be approx. $8,000 in 2021]. And whereas there is money due me from Europe, the receipt of which is doubtful, I therefore direct my Executors to exercise a sound discretion in distributing according to circumstances the residue of my estate as follows: one part or portion to the relief of poor widows and orphans, one other part or portion for masses for the souls of the faithful departed, one other part for the erection of a Catholic Church in the town of Loretto upon the lots above described and one other part to be paid to Susanne Christy, Sarah Durbin, Elizabeth Durbin, Ann Storm, Francis McConnell and Hugh McConnell, all of whom were raised by me" (Penn. Wills, Probate Rec.).

By 1840, it seems as though Stanislaus and his family have moved a few miles from Loretto, PA to Chest Springs, PA in Clearfield Township. One can assume de Daschkopf stayed in Loretto until she died.

In the 1840 US census, Stanislaus Warthon was in Clearfield Township, Cambria County, PA. His name was spelled Stanulas Warton. In 1840, de Daschkopf would still be in Loretto, about 80 years of age.

Ellen, the fifth daughter of de Daschkopf, died September 3, 1844, in Cambria, PA and is buried in St. Michael's Cemetery in Loretto, PA.

In the 1850 U.S. census, "Stanislaus Wharton" was listed as a farmer, age 59, with a value of real estate listed as $2,250 (approx. $75,000 in 2021), with wife Mary, age 56, and four of their children and some grandchildren, living in Clearfield Township, Cambria County, PA.

Finally, in the 1850 U.S. census, there's a census record with de Daschkopf's name and her two daughters on it, even if it has lots of mistakes. The record lists a total population in Loretto of 193 people. Catherine "Whoten," age 58 [we think she'd be closer to 60], Mary, age 56 [we think she'd be 54], and Ann, age 86 [we think she'd be closer to 91], were together in one household. The document said all three were born in Maryland [Ann Warthon was not because she was born in Russia] and all three could not read or write. This probably meant they could not read or write English. We believe they probably would have been well able to read and write German. Maybe the census taker didn't speak German so mistakes were made.

Catherine, the second daughter of de Daschkopf, died in the spring of 1854, in Cambria County, PA, at age 64, and is buried in St. Michael's Cemetery in Loretto, PA.

We have no record of when the third daughter Mary died but we know she was still alive in 1850.

On March 13, 1857, Ann Elizabeth de Daschkopf Warthon died at age 98. She is buried in St. Michaels' Cemetery in Loretto, PA. Her name on the tombstone is written as Ann Wathin.

Her obituary from The Democrat and Sentinel in Ebensburg, PA, ran on Wednesday, April 8, 1857 on page 3 as follows: "On Friday 13th of March, in Loretto, at the residence of her son in-law, John Ivory; Mrs. ANN WHARTON, at the advanced age of 98 years, at her death she had living 7 children, 36 grand children; 54 great grand children, and 3 great great grand children."

> On Friday 13th of March, in Loretto, at the residence of her son in-law, John Ivory; Mrs. ANN WHARTON, at the advanced age of 98 years, at her death she had living 7 children, 36 grand children; 54 great grand children, and 3 great, great grand children.

Obituary of Ann Wharton/Ann Elizabeth de Daschkopf Warthon from the Democrat and Sentinel, Page 3, Ebensburg, Pennsylvania, on Wednesday, April 8, 1857.
http://www.newspapers.com/download/image/?id=71211320&height....

The obituary stated that at her death all seven of her children were living. However, at least two of her seven children predeceased her. Some obituaries are so interesting to read, full of hints behind the basic facts of birth and death, and a list of relatives' names. The reading of this obituary leaves us begging for more. How much we would have loved to see in print the "real and complete story" of de Daschkopf's life.

In the 1860 U.S. census, Stanislaus Wharton was listed as age 69, with his wife and family still owner of their farm in Chest Springs in Clearfield Township in Cambria County, PA. His real estate was valued at $2,000 and his personal estate at $1,200, (approx. $100,000 total in 2021).

In 1861, Stanislaus and his family moved to nearby St. Augustine, after he retired from farming. He opened a grocery store and was appointed postmaster on April 3, 1862.

Theresa, the first daughter of de Daschkopf, died on July 18, 1864 at age 76, in Cambria County, PA. She is buried in St. Michael's Cemetery in Loretto, PA.

On May 10, 1870, Stanislaus' wife, Mary McConnell Warthon/ Wharton, died. She was born about 1792 and is buried in the St. Augustine Cemetery in Loretto, PA in plot #173.

Her obituary, from The Cambria Freeman (Ebensburg, PA) ran on Thursday, June 2, 1870, on page 3 as follows: "WHARTON. At St. Augustine, Cambria County, Pa., on May 19th, 1870, MARY, wife of Stanislaus Wharton, in the 77th year of her age. The deceased was a native of Emmitsburg, Md., and came to the Allegheny Mountains in 1807. For several years she was an inmate of the household of the venerable Prince Gallitzin, by whom she was nurtured in those sentiments of Christian piety which marked the course of her useful life. She and her husband were among the early settlers at the Loop, now St. Augustine. Their union was blessed by numerous offspring, and her mortal remains were followed to the grave by her children's children to the fourth generation. The funeral took place on May 12th, from St. Augustine Church. During her brief mortal illness her patience and resignation were a striking proof that a blameless, pious life is the best preparation for a happy death. May she rest in peace."

In the 1870 U.S. census, "Stany" Wharton was listed as age 78 in Clearfield Township with his daughter, Alice, and with other relatives near-by. He still owned a considerable estate.

In January of 1873, Stanislaus Warthon died in St Augustine, PA. He is buried in St. Augustine Cemetery. His daughter, Alice, was appointed postmaster of St. Augustine the following month.

A reading of the Last Will and Testament of Stanislaus Wharton, dated August 19, 1872, and some accompanying documents show the dispersal of his goods, the names of his family members, and bills to be paid. A very thorough list of the contents of his house and grocery store provide a slice of life representative of rural Pennsylvania in the mid to late 1800s. He left cash amounts to all of his children or grand children but all of his personal possessions and the contents of the grocery store were willed to his daughter, Alice (Cambria County, PA archives). She was living in his house, had taken care of her father, and even inherited his position as postmaster of St. Augustine.

From all of the above references and facts, we believe it is clear that Ann Elizabeth de Daschkopf Warthon, and her large family, were closely linked to Father Demetrius Gallitzin.

The following pages contain photos of Cambria County, PA during the time that Ann Elizabeth de Daschkopf and Father Demetrius Gallitzin lived there. *University of St. Michael's College Library, Cresson PA. Swope Bros, Printers October 10, 1899 "Souvenir of Loretto Centenary 1799-1899" Public Domain. https://ia801405.us.archive.org/28/items/souvenirloretto00unknuoft/souvenirloretto00unkn-uoft.pdf*

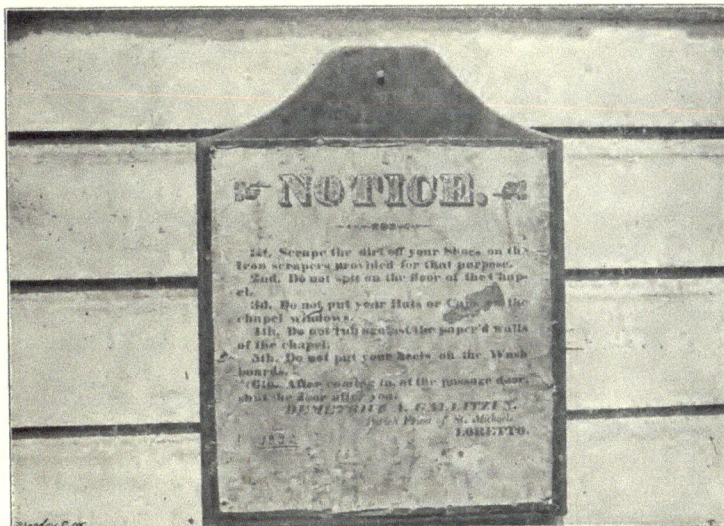

THE ORIGINAL NOTICE AND BOARD ARE STILL PRESERVED.

NOTICE.

I. Scrape the dirt off your shoes on the iron scrapers provided for that purpose.

II. Do not spit on the floor of the chapel.

III. Do not put your hats and caps on the chapel windows.

IV. Do not rub against the papered walls of the chapel.

V. Do not put your heels on the washboards.

VI. After coming in at the passage door shut the door after you.   DEMETRIUS AUGUSTINE GALLITZIN,
                                        Parish Priest of Loretto.

Gallitzin's original notice and signboard was still intact in 1899. The list sets forth rules to be followed by any who entered his house (193).

FIRST MEETING OF FATHER LEMKE AND FATHER GALLITZIN. SEPTEMBER, 1834.

By 1834, Gallitzin could no longer travel on horseback because of a bad fall. He also had trouble walking and since wagons toppled over easily on poor roads, he chose to use a sled/sledge year round, drawn by two strong horses (279). He found this the safest and most efficient way to travel many miles to visit his parishioners.

THE OLD PARRISH HOMESTEAD, WHERE FATHER GALLITZIN USED TO HOLD "STATIONS."

For Catholics who lived too far away from Loretto, Gallitzin made regular journeys to say mass to them. In the book, there is an account by a visiting priest, Father Lemcke, during a visit with Gallitzin to the rural home of the Parrish family, in September of 1834: "The Catholics of the neighborhood were already assembled …around the house in which an altar was put up, its principle materials having been taken from the sled. Gallitzin then sat down in one corner to hear confessions…After mass, at which Gallitzin preached and when a few children had been baptized, the altar was taken away, and the dinner table set in its place" (279, 280).

THE HITCHING GROUNDS.   AFTER MASS ON SUNDAY.

When Gallitzin was home, services were given in St. Michael's Church. Those who lived near enough walked or traveled there by horseback or wagon (241).

THE TOMB OF FATHER GALLITZIN.   ERECTED 1847.

This modest tomb was originally between the church and Gallitzin's home. In 1899, his remains were reburied in a new crypt and the crypt topped by a life-sized statue. A new church was built on the site of the original churches. Nearby today is a chapel which adjoins Gallitzin's original "new" house, constructed in the 1830s. It contains his bed, a clock and desk, his violin, a silver chalice and vestments made by his mother from her wedding dress ("Prince Gallitzin's Tomb" from dojohnstown.com October 27, 2014) (59).

VI.

Facts:

How
Catherine the Great
and
Father Demetrius Gallitzin
Were Connected

Catherine the Great ruled Russia from 1762-1796, even though she was neither Russian by birth, nor a member of the Romanov family ("Cath. the Great").

Demetrius Gallitzin was born in The Hague, the Netherlands, on December 22, 1770 while his father was a Russian ambassador there. His father, Prince Dmitrii Golitsyn, was one of a long line of his family to serve Russian rulers since the 13th century. Prince Golitsyn also served Russia in Italy and Paris where he became close friends with Voltaire and Diderot. He was friends, too, with Benjamin Franklin, with whom he exchanged ideas and theories on electricity ("Cause for..." part 2).

His mother, Adelheid Amalie von Schmettau, was a Prussian countess. She was raised as a Catholic but she and her husband raised their children in the Russian Orthodox religion ("Cause for..." part 2, 4).

In 1772, to avoid a plague throughout Russia, Catherine the Great toured Europe and visited The Hague. She was there for Demetrius' baptism into the Russian Orthodox Church and served as his godmother ("Cause for..." part 1). As she held Demetrius in her arms, she appointed him an officer of the guard (Brownson 16).

A Dutch prince, husband of Gallitzin's mother's friend, owned a country house on the road between the Hague and the town of Sheveningen, a fishing village on the North Sea. Gallitzin and his parents and sister moved to a neighboring house in 1774. Here, young Prince Demetrius played with peasant children and fishermen's children, and the children of the Dutch rulers. This was the first time Demetrius was "exposed to the world of trees, farms and flowers and began to learn the laws of nature" ("Cause for..." part 1).

His mother also took him and his sister to visit Germany although never Russia. The language spoken at home was French but he became fluent in German ("Dem. A. Gallitzin").

In 1786, Demetrius' mother, after following the Russian Orthodox religion, the religion of the Russian aristocracy for years, returned to Catholicism and by 1787, Demetrius, and his sister, Mimi/Marian, became Catholic, too. Under Russian law, no Catholic could inherit titles or estates or hold office in Russia. After his father's death, he received very little of his inheritance ("Dem. A. Gallitzin").

VII.

Facts:

The Children
of
Catherine the Great

Here we discuss the facts about the pregnancies and births of the known children of Catherine the Great, who was married throughout these times to Peter III. Peter was pretty much assuredly not the father of any of these children, according to many accounts over the centuries. Catherine needed to convince her husband, and others, that he was the father in hopes that her/their children would be in line to inherit the Russian throne.

FIRST CHILD: GRAND DUKE PAUL PETROVICH

Catherine's husband Peter was immature, holding a lifelong love for all things Prussian. He had survived a series of serious childhood illnesses which left him sterile, but not impotent, but he had little interest in a sexual relationship with Catherine once they were married (Oldenbourg 155).

Court members were crude and uneducated, there was filth and debauchery everywhere, and Peter and his wife, Catherine, were treated poorly and kept apart from their friends. Peter played with his wooden soldiers, planning imaginary battle strategies, while Catherine rode her horse in the fresh air and read her books (Troyat 63-66, 68-71).

At age 26, Peter was still a virgin. Catherine met Serge Saltykov in 1752, when she was 23 and still a virgin. Saltykov, Catherine's first of many lovers, was from one of Russia's oldest and noblest families (Troyat 79).

On December 14, 1752 Catherine had a miscarriage and another one in May (or June) of 1753 (Oldenbourg 156, 161). Nine years after Catherine and Peter had married a third pregnancy was successful. When Catherine became pregnant with Saltykov's child it was imperative that Peter have an operation that would allow him to begin sexual relations with Catherine to deflect the parentage of the child. His simple operation, phimosis, releasing his foreskin, was a success (Troyat 82) (Oldenbourg 154).

Catherine gave birth to Grand Duke PAUL PETROVICH on September 20, 1754. Paul was probably the son of Serge Saltykov but was given the name Petrovich to imply he was the "son of Peter." Saltykov was never told of his fatherhood. Shortly after the birth, Saltykov was sent away as Russian ambassador to Hamburg, and later to Paris and Dresden, and he and Catherine never saw each other again (Troyat 88, 93).

Shortly after he was born, Paul was taken from Catherine into the care of Empress Elizabeth and Catherine was essentially abandoned to fend for herself, left uncleaned and unattended, her job of producing an heir completed (Troyat 89). Catherine didn't seem to have too much expectation or desire to raise any of her children. Russian parents of nobility rarely had a part in the raising of their children (Woronzoff-Dashkoff 79). It wasn't until 40 days later that she saw her son Paul again, briefly (91), and rarely saw him after that until he was nearly eight years old (Cronin 202).

He was accepted as Peter's son, brought up in the Winter Palace, and married twice. He became Emperor of Russia in 1796 and was murdered in St. Michael's Castle in 1801 ("Cath. the Great").

SECOND CHILD: ANNA PETROVNA

In 1755, England sent an ambassador to Russia, Charles Hanbury-Williams, hoping to strengthen a Russian-English alliance against France. Too old himself to hope for Catherine's attention and knowing her "weakness for handsome men" he introduced her to a member of his staff, Count Stanislaus Augustus Poniatowski, from an illustrious Polish family. Poniatowski had spent most of his life in foreign countries and right before he met Catherine had lived in Paris. Three years younger than Catherine, Poniatowski fell madly in love with her and never loved anyone else the rest of his life (Troyat 95-98). The two of them oddly even spent social time with Peter and his mistress, Elizabeth Vorontsova, the crude and much less educated sister of Ekaterina Vorontsova Dashkova (Oldenbourg 183, 184) (Troyat 101).

By the middle of 1758, Catherine was again pregnant and most assumed it was Poniatowski's child. Empress Elizabeth had been ill, and there was a lot of court intrigue as to who would succeed her on the throne. Catherine was hoping it would be her, and not her husband Peter, or her young son Paul (Troyat 101-103).

On the night of December 8/9, 1758, with the Empress Elizabeth and Peter there while she was in labor, Catherine gave birth to a daughter in the Winter Palace. Catherine wanted to name the baby Elizabeth to honor the Empress but the Empress wanted her to be named Anna, after her older sister, who was also Peter's mother. ANNA PETROVNA was taken away immediately to the Empress' quarters, as had happened with Paul (Troyat 107-108) (Oldenbourg 193-194).

Poniatowski spent time with Catherine following Anna's birth and didn't leave for Poland until much later (Oldenbourg 194).

Shortly after the birth, the child was baptized and Elizabeth served as godmother; she held Anna above the baptismal font and brought Catherine, who did not witness any of the celebrations, and Peter a gift of 60,000 rubles. Elizabeth took Anna and raised the baby herself, as she had done with Paul. (Troyat 108)

[Note: A number of different dates were given for Anna Petrovna's birth: Catherine was pregnant in the spring 1757, and she gave birth on December 9, 1757 (Cronin 111). The birth was late 1757 or early 1758 (Oldenbourg 194). The night of December 8/9, 1758 was the time of the birth (Troyat 107). The most alluring reference to the exact birthdate of Anna Petrovna comes from Catherine the Great's own memoirs for 1758: "At the end of September we returned to the city. As I began to grow heavy because of my pregnancy, I appeared no more in public, believing that I was closer to giving birth than I really was." (Cruse & Hoogenboom, 299) "In the night of December 8 to 9, I began to feel labor pains." (Cruse & Hoogenboom, 301) "I gave birth on December 9 between ten and eleven at night to a girl..."(Cruse & Hoogenboom, 302) "Six days later the Empress held this child over the baptismal font..." (Cruse & Hoogenboom, 302) There's some discrepancy in her death dates as well. For the purposes of our story, it seems to make sense to use the official church records inscribed on the child's tombstone, which notes her death date as March 8, 1759.]

Description of the baptism ceremony of Grand Duchess Anna Petrovna on December 17, 1757. *(This date doesn't agree with Catherine's own memoirs.)* *By Unknown - http://romanovy.rusarchives.ru/petr-3/opisanie-tseremonii-kreshcheniya-velikoi-knyazhny-anny-petrovny.html, Public Domain, https://commons.wikimedia.org/w/index.php?curid=38199336*

From the time she was a few months old, Anna was brought up miles from her mother, in the Imperial Palace of Peterhof, while Catherine lived for awhile at the Grand Duke's Palace of Oranienbaum, 20 versts/14 miles away. Both of these palaces near the seaside overlooking the Gulf of Finland, and not far from St. Petersburg, had been built for Peter the Great in the early 1700's. Anna, and her older brother, Paul, were in the daily care of nurse maids and nannies and other servants who answered to the Empress Elizabeth (Oldenbourg 213).

There was continual court intrigue as to Empress Elizabeth's successor, and Catherine was essentially accused of treason. Needing to gain Elizabeth's favor, Catherine offered to leave the country and go back to Germany, saying that since she never saw her children, even when she lived in the same house with them, it was a matter of indifference to her whether she were near them or far away (Troyat 112). During a later meeting, the Empress showed pity for Catherine and her situation regarding her children and set up a time when Catherine could see her children (Troyat 118).

Even though Catherine eventually received permission to visit the children once a week, there was little opportunity for them to bond with each other (Oldenbourg 213).

When Catherine finally met with five year old Paul and Anna, only a few months old, she felt as though they were strangers to her and the little ones were confused about this unfamiliar person, too. Catherine played with them while nurses and governesses looked on. She had very little maternal feelings toward them and felt as though she had produced them solely for Elizabeth's benefit (Troyat 118). Oldenbourg says Anna is four months old at this meeting (210).

Cronin paints a much sweeter picture of Catherine. "At last Catherine enjoyed to a limited degree the joys of motherhood. She watched little Paul, aged four, as he played in the Palace garden, and pretty Anna, aged nearly one, begin to crawl" (123).

[Note the different ages given for Anna by the three authors.] After this short time with her children, Catherine had a rather personal meeting with Elizabeth, who wanted to know more about Catherine's love affairs with Saltykov and Poniatowski, about her poor relations with her husband, Peter, and about the true paternity of the two children, Paul and Anna. During this private talk, the Empress began to understand the situation with Catherine's marriage so she compromised and set up some more rules for visiting the children. Catherine liked the tone of the conversation and the improvement in their friendship (Cronin 120).

Even though the Empress finally understood Catherine's poor relationship with her husband and Peter's very odd behaviors, and why Catherine looked elsewhere for love and companionship, Poniatowski was expelled from Russia. More so than any other reason, Empress Elizabeth was upset that he was Catholic and banished him from Russia (Cronin 120). Oldenbourg suggests that "the young Princess Anne, Stanislaus' daughter, died... not long after the handsome Pole's departure" (213), which she said took place at the end of 1758 (194). Troyat seems to make a more sensible time line. "In April 1759, a few weeks after her lover's departure, she lost the daughter she had by him, little Princess Anna" (119). In any case, both authors agree that the child died not too long after Poniatowski set off for Poland.

In her memoirs, Catherine made no mention of Anna's death on March 8, 1759, which probably happened at Peterhof Palace, 14 miles from St. Petersburg. But Catherine was "inconsolable and entered into a state of shock" ("List of Gd. Duchesses"). Anna's funeral took place on March 15, 1759, at the St. Alexander Nevsky Lavra Monastery in St. Petersburg, where she is also buried. After the funeral, Catherine never mentioned her dead daughter again ("Cath. the Great").

On Anna Petrovna's tombstone, her death date is given as March 8, 1759 (the birth date on her tombstone is a mystery and doesn't agree with any of the reference books that we've researched). After the passing of more than two centuries and considering that some dates may have been purposely recorded wrong, one can see the difficulty in establishing exact dates for the birth and death of Anna Petrovna and the date Poniatowski returned to Poland. For the purposes of our story we have tried to be true to the range of suggested dates for these events.

View of the Large Cascade and Peterhof Palace, December 31, 1836.

By Ivan Aivazovsky - http://aivazovski.ru/gal301/, Public Domain, https://commons.wiki-media.org/w/index.php?curid=18257263

Oranienbaum Palace, Russia, where Catherine sometimes lived when Anna Petrovna was a baby.

By Unknown - http://lomonosov.municip.ru/photos/gorod-i-lyudi/priglashenie-v-oranien-baum/01-oranienbaum-1900_km_175.jpg/view, Public Domain, https://commons.wikimedia.org/w/index.php?curid=13554746

БЛАГОВѢРНАЯ ГОСУДАРЫНЯ ВЕЛИКАЯ КНЯЖ[

АННА ПЕТРОВНА

ДЩЕРЬ ГОСУДАРЯ ВЕЛИКАГО КНЯЗЯ

ПЕТРА ѲЕОДОРОВИЧА

РОДИЛАСЬ 1757 ГОДА МАРТА 8 ДНЯ

СКОНЧАЛАСЬ 1759 ГОДА МАРТА 8 ДНЯ

Tombstone of Grand Duchess Anna Petrovna in the Church of the
Annunciation of the Alexander Nevsky Lavra (1757-1759). *(A lot of information
on this tombstone does not line up with Catherine's own memoirs).*

THIRD CHILD: COUNT ALEXEI BOBRINSKY

Since Empress Elizabeth was dying and the throne was about to be vacant, Catherine wanted to ensure she would be the next ruler, not her husband or her son. She knew she needed to build allegiance with the soldiers, giving her military backing in case of a coup. She also wanted a new lover. She chose Gregory Orlov, one of five brothers, all of them soldiers devoted to the Russian throne (Troyat 129). He was handsome but had "only a mediocre mind and very little education" (Troyat 123).

By the time of Empress Elizabeth's death, Catherine was five months pregnant with Orlov's child. She kept this pregnancy secret and hidden using tight clothes to hold her in until she could no longer hide it. She pretended to have sprained her ankle and could not leave her room, allowing her to wear flowing clothes, with her foot bandaged and her face tired looking. She was cared for by one trusted and experienced maid and her faithful valet Chkurin, who would have given his life for her. As she was ready to give birth, to distract those who lived in the palace who might hear birth pains, Chkurin set his own house on fire, knowing Peter, who loved fires, and his group, would all rush out to watch the spectacle. The plan worked (Troyat 137).

On April 11, 1762, with the house (the Winter Palace) empty, Catherine, with the help of her servant, gave birth to a son. As soon as he had been washed and swaddled, he was "taken from his mother by Chkurin, who carried him off rolled up in a beaver blanket, to the arms of a waiting female relative" (Troyat 138). This baby, later baptized ALEXEI, became Count

Bobrinsky. This made-up name "Bobrinsky" comes from the Russian word, "bobre," or beaver. For the third time, a child of hers was taken away right at the start, but Catherine had "avoided a scandal" (Troyat 138). Another account said it was Catherine who wrapped Alexei in a beaverskin and sent him away to the country, to live with foster parents (Cronin 137).

Alexei Bobrinsky was later brought up in the Imperial Palace and studied in Paris. He died June 20, 1813. It is believed that Catherine had other children with Gregory Orlov (Cronin 322).

OTHER POSSIBLE CHILDREN

Nobody seems to know exactly how many children Catherine the Great had. In 1774, 12 years after her child Alexei was born, Gregory Potemkin became Catherine's lover. He may have been the only one of her many lovers that she actually married, and referred to him in correspondence as her husband (Cronin 216). Elizabeth Grigoryevna Temkina (July 13, 1775-May 25, 1854) is thought to be the daughter of that relationship ("List of Gd. Duchesses").

VIII.

Our Theories:
The Missing Years

Our story of Ann Elizabeth de Daschkopf's true identity is intriguing. From our research, and from gathering all of the facts you've just read, we've concluded that de Daschkopf and Anna Petrovna are the same person. Our book could stop here—and our theory proved—just based upon these facts. But we've gone a little further and have had a lot of fun weaving together what we know, with what we don't know, to come up with our own theories to account for the "missing years" (from her disappearance in St. Petersburg in 1759 until her marriage in Philadelphia in 1786 at about age 30).

In the following theories, we consider the people who might have taken responsibility for de Daschkopf and brought her to safety. We try to figure out how she spent her childhood years, where she was as a young adult, and how and why she came to America. In doing so, we hope to show how a select group of rather important people (surely with the help of nameless others) could have kept track of her and protected her until she was old enough to be on her own. We hope that readers of this book will help us fill in these missing years with the true facts.

THEORY ONE
"End of the Story?"

Perhaps Anna Petrovna, child of Catherine the Great, really did die. If our history books are correct, we don't need any theories or this book. That would be the end of our connection to Russian history. However, if true, we still need an explanation of how and why Gallitzin had such an affinity for de Daschkopf when she lived in his missionary community of Loretto, PA.

THEORY TWO
"Years in Poland and The Hague"

Assuming that Catherine the Great's daughter did not die, theory two presents a strong and romantic case for upholding our belief that Anna Petrovna and de Daschkopf are the same person.

Since Catherine had not grown attached to her children (especially baby Anna) and since Paul was accepted as her husband Peter's child even though he wasn't, and since Anna would be in a dangerous situation because of her illegitimacy, perhaps Empress Elizabeth and Catherine made an agreement during their frank conversation in 1759 about Catherine, her children and her lovers. If the baby wasn't a legitimate descendant of Peter, and the Russian people knew that, they wouldn't accept Anna as having claim to the throne.

Armed with the knowledge that Poniatowski was Catholic and not Russian Orthodox (and perhaps that he posed a threat to the legitimacy of children born to Catherine) Empress Elizabeth banished him from Russia and sent him to Poland. Maybe she figured out that since baby Anna needed to be removed from Russia, along with Poniatowski, and thinking that a simple way to make someone vanish is to have her "die," Elizabeth set the wheels in motion. Perhaps loyal and faithful servants who were in on the plan sent word that Anna was ill and afterward announced that she had suddenly died. Catherine could have been instructed to act devastated and never mention her child again. And perhaps she obliged, afraid she would reveal too much if she spoke of her. Maybe a substitution was then made for the baby, a funeral was arranged and the substitution was buried in a monastery near-by.

Meantime, since Poniatowski was headed hundreds of miles away it would make sense to involve him in the care of his child, especially since he loved Catherine so much. (40 years later he said he never stopped loving her.) Maybe with the assistance of Ekaterina Dashkova, a close friend of Catherine's at the time, Poniatowski waited in the countryside southwest of St. Petersburg until the baby arrived. Maybe faithful servants cared for the baby as they traveled with him to Poland. Once there, under the protection of her father, she could have been placed in the home of a family member who raised her. Maybe she was baptized once again, this time into the Catholic faith (the faith of her father) and given the Christian name of Catherine (as Gallitzin called her later in life). Poniatowski might have chosen this name to honor his first and only love. Maybe this was when Anna was given a new last name as well—not Poniatowski but de Daschkopf (with a German spelling) to deflect attention to her parentage and country of her birth. Perhaps the name de Daschkopf came from Mikhail Dashkov, the husband of Catherine's friend, and in thanks, Catherine made Dashkov a Russian Field Marshall in Poland, ultimately becoming the person in charge of placing Poniatowski on the Polish throne.

If Anna were now named Catherine de Daschkopf, she could have spent many safe and happy years as a minor noble in Poland. When Ekaterina Dashkova toured Europe in 1775, years after her husband's death, she could have visited with Poniatowski and his daughter. During this time, she might have sensed

Poniatowski's reign was weakening as Poland had begun to be partitioned by other countries. If she felt the young woman's safety was at stake, perhaps she contacted their friends, the Golitsyns, in The Hague, to offer assistance. (The elder Prince Golitsyn was Russian ambassador there, which would have been a safe and comforting connection for everyone.) It was then that Catherine de Daschkopf could have left Poland, saying goodbye to the man she might not have known was her true father, and was welcomed in The Hague.

She could have spent her later teens and early twenties there with the Golitsyn family. Maybe she was a governess to the Golitsyn children, a young boy (Demetrius Gallitzin) and girl, or perhaps she was a higher level servant. She could have learned how to weave and spin there, helping to pay back the hospitality that was given to her. Thirteen years of age separated young Demetrius and de Daschkopf but she would have had ample time to get to know him during her stay. The Golitsyns were an educated and intellectual family who spoke many languages and could have taught her a lot.

During those years, Catherine the Great might have kept track of her daughter through correspondence with Prince Golitsyn, her ambassador from Russia (since we know she had previously traveled to The Hague to escape a plague raging in Russia and was also Gallitzin's godmother).

Poniatowski also could have kept track of his daughter this way since both he and the Golitsyns served Russia and were from old nobility.

THEORY THREE
"Ekaterina Dashkova Keeps Track of the Child"

The relationship between Catherine the Great and Ekaterina Dashkova varied over the years. At times they were close friends, yet at other times Catherine used her power against her. But since we are assuming that Anna did not really die in 1759 but had a secret existence elsewhere, then it's plausible that Catherine would have confided in her friend about the dangerous situation that her baby was in. Catherine may have asked Dashkova's help in finding safe places for her baby to live since Dashkova had a wide range of friends scattered throughout Europe. She kept up a steady stream of correspondence with many of them; others she visited in person. Dashkova could have been an intermediary when needed, finding sanctuary, checking on the child's health and safety over the years, relaying information to Catherine, Poniatowski or to Gallitzin.

With such a wide range of connections, Dashkova could have had many opportunities to keep track of the child and to make sure all was well. If one looks into more detail at the people and places visited by Dashkova on her two European journeys, one in 1769-1771 (Woronzoff-Dashkoff 97-104, 113-118) and one in 1775-1782 (125-149), it's possible that her interconnections were more than just coincidences. Maybe, instead of just getting away from Catherine and stimulating her intellect, her ulterior motive to travel was also to check up on Catherine's daughter, who would have been in her early teens and twenties by then. One can imagine that even before the years Dashkova traveled, she would have been communicating by letter about her concerns and interests to her wide range of connections, including Catherine.

Dashkova's friends and acquaintances were also connected to each other and all moved in the same circles so there could be a possibility that they discussed the child secretly among themselves. And if de Daschkopf went anywhere in Europe during the years of the 1760s and 1770s, it would seem likely that this closely connected group of people could have kept track of her and maybe even kept in touch with her personally.

Dashkova also had family members who served in the Russian government and she knew a number of ambassadors appointed by the Russian monarchy. Her friend Prince Dmitrii Golitsyn was connected with Catherine the Great, Diderot, Benjamin Franklin, and his son, Demetrius Gallitzin. Dashkova also knew a diplomat who had been involved with Poniatowski's placement as the King of Poland. Even earlier, when Dashkova made her first European trip, her guide and advisor was a cousin who had been a Russian diplomat to The Hague.

In 1770-1771, Dashkova became friends with Diderot in Paris. In 1773, Diderot spent three months with the Golitsyns in The Hague on his way to Russia to visit with Catherine. Perhaps they discussed their mutual friend, Dashkova, or perhaps Diderot brought Catherine word of her daughter's where-abouts with information he might have learned from the Golitsyn family.

In 1776, Dashkova visited Poniatowski in Warsaw. "She often met with Stanislas-Augustine Poniatowski, the last king of Poland

and Catherine's second lover. Dashkova admired him for his kindness, intellect, and interest in the arts but she felt he was ill suited to be king" (Woronzoff-Dashkoff 126). In a letter dated October 9, 1776, Poniatowski thanked her for some art prints she had given him (126). It's fun to think that when Dashkova visited with Poniatowski, his daughter de Daschkopf, now a young woman, might have been there, too.

When both Dashkova and Catherine were in Europe about the same time they may have met up together at The Hague, where they were hosted by the Golitsyns. Maybe the child was living there at the time. Imagine the conversations if that were the case.

Benjamin Franklin and Ekaterina Dashkova also had a strong mutual admiration for each other's intellect. Franklin was friends with Bishop John Carroll, of Baltimore, MD, who in turn was a mentor and a friend to Father Demetrius Gallitzin. Franklin and Prince Golitsyn, Demetrius' Gallitzin's father, were both fascinated by electricity and kept up correspondence about new scientific discoveries in that field (Woronzoff-Dashkoff 171). Imagine the ways these people all could have shared knowledge of de Daschkopf with each other, both in Europe and in America, since they knew each other.

In 1780, Dashkova visited The Hague. In her memoirs, Dashkova mentioned Prince Golitsyn several times and spoke fondly of his sense of humor (151-153). At the time of this visit, de Daschkopf would have been in her mid-twenties and Gallitzin about ten years old. One wonders if de Daschkopf and Dashkova were known to each other and if they had conversations. Did

Gallitzin have a memory of this visit in his later years, when he discovered de Daschkopf's true identity in America?

It's intriguing to think of all of the many ways that Dashkova and her friends and acquaintances could have kept track of de Daschkopf during her "missing years."

THEORY FOUR
"Variation of Theory Two: Years in Germany"

De Daschkopf may have been brought up in Germany, not in Poland and The Hague, with the initial assistance of loyal servants and then placed in the care of distant relatives of Catherine.

De Daschkopf could not have been taken away to be brought up by Catherine's immediate family because Catherine's mother died in Paris, broke, at age 40, in 1760 and Catherine's brother, Fritz, died young (Oldenbourg 373, 374).

If one assumes that de Daschkopf was sent to live in Germany with someone else almost immediately after birth, and was probably in Germany her whole life until coming to America, it may be that she met Gallitzin in Germany. Each summer Gallitzin's mother would take him and his sister traveling to major cities around Germany so they could learn the geography and history of the area. This was where Gallitzin became fluent in German since the family spoke French at home ("Dem. A. Gallitzin"). Perhaps Catherine had requested Gallitzin's mother to look into how her daughter was doing.

THEORY FIVE
"The Name de Daschkopf: Part 1"

From the start of our research, we have wondered about the origin of the name de Daschkopf. We believe there's a possibility that Ekaterina Dashkova and her husband, Mikhail Dashkov, had a close tie to this. On the very first page of Dashkova's Memoirs she began, "I was born in St. Petersburg...The Empress Elizaveta had just returned from Moscow, where she had been for her coronation. She held me at the baptismal font, while the Grand Duke, known afterward under the name of Emperor Peter III, was my godfather" (Dashkova 31).

Just as Empress Elizabeth was godmother to Ekaterina Vorontso-va-Dashkova, she was also godmother to Catherine's daughter, Anna Petrovna. Therefore, a godmother/godchild bond could have formed early on between them. However, months before Anna's birth, Elizabeth was overweight and suffered from convulsions which left her cold and unconscious for hours. She was not expected to live long (Cronin 102). Because of her ill health she might have been concerned for the future care of Anna after her death so decided to act quickly to make other arrangements.

Even though we have little information about the details made between Catherine and Empress Elizabeth, we know that they had a long conversation in 1759 to discuss a change in visitations between Catherine and her children. Perhaps one of the decisions made was that Anna "would die" (as far as the public perceived it) and that Elizabeth would instead turn the baby over to the care and safety of her beloved godchild Ekaterina

Dashkova, now a young woman who was friends with Catherine. If the Dashkovs agreed to raise the child in their household after Empress Elizabeth died in 1762 (possibly as an orphaned cousin or a poor relative) or helped to smuggle baby Anna out of the country (perhaps to The Hague, Poland or Germany) they would have also been expected to give their name to the child. There would have been a risk to Dashkova's reputation and to that of her new husband, Mikhail Dashkov, if others were to find out, but maybe because they were young and brave, they agreed.

They also could have agreed because they knew there was an opportunity for reward. Catherine had been known to reward her lovers (and confidants) with high positions. Dashkov was made Russian Field Marshall at the young age of 26. Was he rewarded for giving his family name and precious time to Anna? In her memoirs, Dashkova wrote that Catherine "spoke highly of my husband and called him 'her little Field-Marshall'" (Dashkova 112). Shortly afterward, Dashkov was given the responsibility to place Poniatowski (coincidentally the baby's father) on the Polish throne. This position unfortunately led to Dashkov's illness and death, and Ekaterina became a young widow with two of her own young children in her care. Nevertheless, Anna might have been safe with her new identity that linked her to the large Dashkov family and not to her birth mother.

THEORY SIX
"The Name de Daschkopf: Part 2"

There is another, and one would think, obvious possibility for the name de Daschkopf. Catherine the Great and Mikhail Dashkov might have had an affair in the window of time between Catherine's affair with Poniatowski (and the birth of Anna Petrovna in December of 1758) and her affair with Orlov (and the birth of Alexei in April 1762). Dashkov was not sent away as Field Marshall in Poland until 1762. However, in all accounts of Catherine's life, her memoirs and her many biographies, Dashkov's name is never even suggested as her lover and seems only to be linked to Ekaterina Vorontsova.

THEORY SEVEN
"A New Life in America"

The above theories have concerned de Daschkopf's earliest years in Russia and Europe but this theory helps to fill in the blanks of her life as a young adult in America. One has to consider why and how it came to be that she left Europe and sailed to America.

There is disagreement about a lot of the information regarding the life of the man de Daschkopf married. We believe Joseph Warthon was of German origin (and not a British red-coat named John Wharton, descended from the Whartons of Wharton Hall in England). The name in particular was always spelled Warthon in earlier documents and only changed in spelling when their son Stanislaus became a young man.

In the absence of any proof, one possible scenario involves the Golitsyns of The Hague. Gallitzin's mother (Princess Golitsyn) frequently took her daughter and son on trips throughout Germany to explore the larger cities and become acquainted with German culture. Perhaps de Daschkopf accompanied them, becoming increasingly adept in the German language, and during one of those trips met a handsome German by the name of Joseph Warthon.

After she met Joseph, maybe she told him the strange details of her unlikely past and they decided it would be safest for her to make a new life, and her own new beginning, in America, away from Russia and Europe. At this time, she might have had to say goodbye to the relative security of those who had raised and protected her as well as say goodbye to the Golitsyn children. At this time, she probably thought that she would never see her childhood friend, Prince Demetrius Gallitzin, ever again.

Perhaps de Daschkopf and Warthon sailed to Philadelphia where they were married in a simple church ceremony in 1786. And then after realizing that Philadelphia was crowded, and there was more promise of religious toleration for Catholics in Maryland, they might have moved there when it was time to start a family. De Daschkopf could have named their first son Stanislaus, to honor her birth father, Stanislaus Poniatowski, the last King of Poland.

We know that somewhere in her years in Maryland while raising their seven children she reconnected again with Gallitzin, now a Catholic missionary serving in Maryland. They may have met during his early mission trip to Port Tobacco, in Charles County, MD or later on one of his "circuit rider" trips throughout the state. Maybe they didn't recognize each other right away since so many years had passed and neither of them ever expected their paths to cross again. De Daschkopf might have only realized that the priest who was known to her as Father Smith was actually her childhood friend Prince Demetrius Gallitzin when the Pennsylvania legislature allowed him to resume using his birth name in 1809. Maybe that's why the Warthon family, minus Joseph who had died, headed to Loretto right after that announcement to be near him for the rest of their lives.

THEORY EIGHT
"DNA Proof"

Another theory might not be necessary if new official and factual records turn up or if our family is able to compare our DNA samples with the known ancestors of Catherine the Great, or even of Stanislaus Poniatowski. Maybe the next generation will have that chance.

IS THIS THE REAL FAMILY TREE?

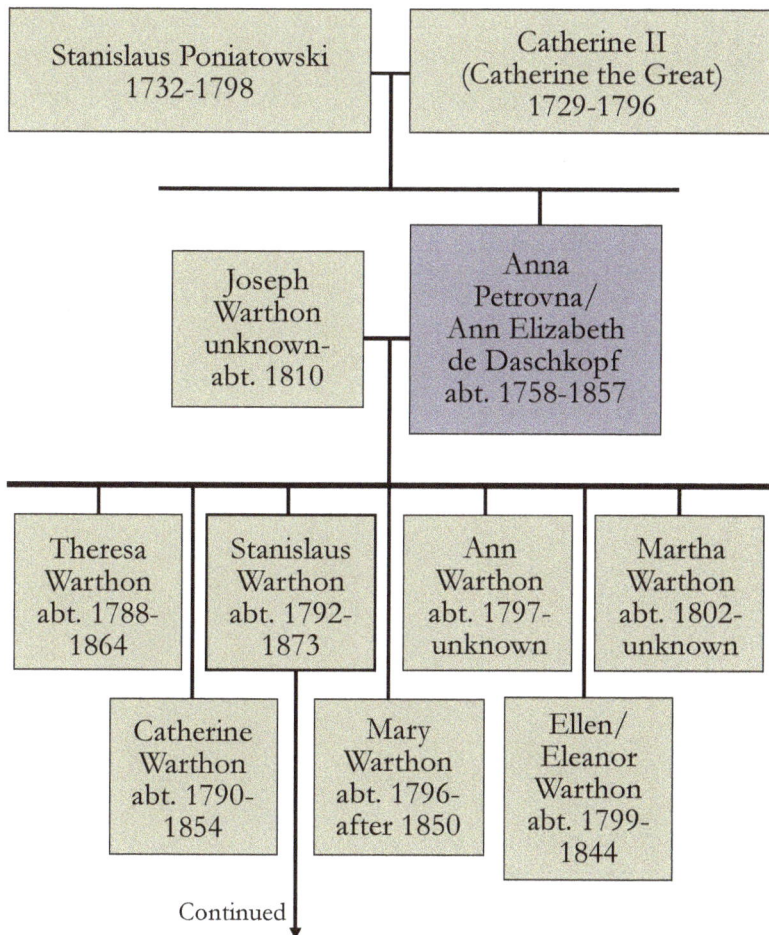

```
Stanislaus Poniatowski          Catherine II
1732-1798                       (Catherine the Great)
                                1729-1796
```

```
Joseph                          Anna
Warthon                         Petrovna/
unknown-                        Ann Elizabeth
abt. 1810                       de Daschkopf
                                abt. 1758-1857
```

```
Theresa       Stanislaus        Ann             Martha
Warthon       Warthon           Warthon         Warthon
abt. 1788-    abt. 1792-        abt. 1797-      abt. 1802-
1864          1873              unknown         unknown
```

```
    Catherine          Mary             Ellen/
    Warthon            Warthon           Eleanor
    abt. 1790-         abt. 1796-       Warthon
    1854               after 1850       abt. 1799-
                                        1844
```

Continued

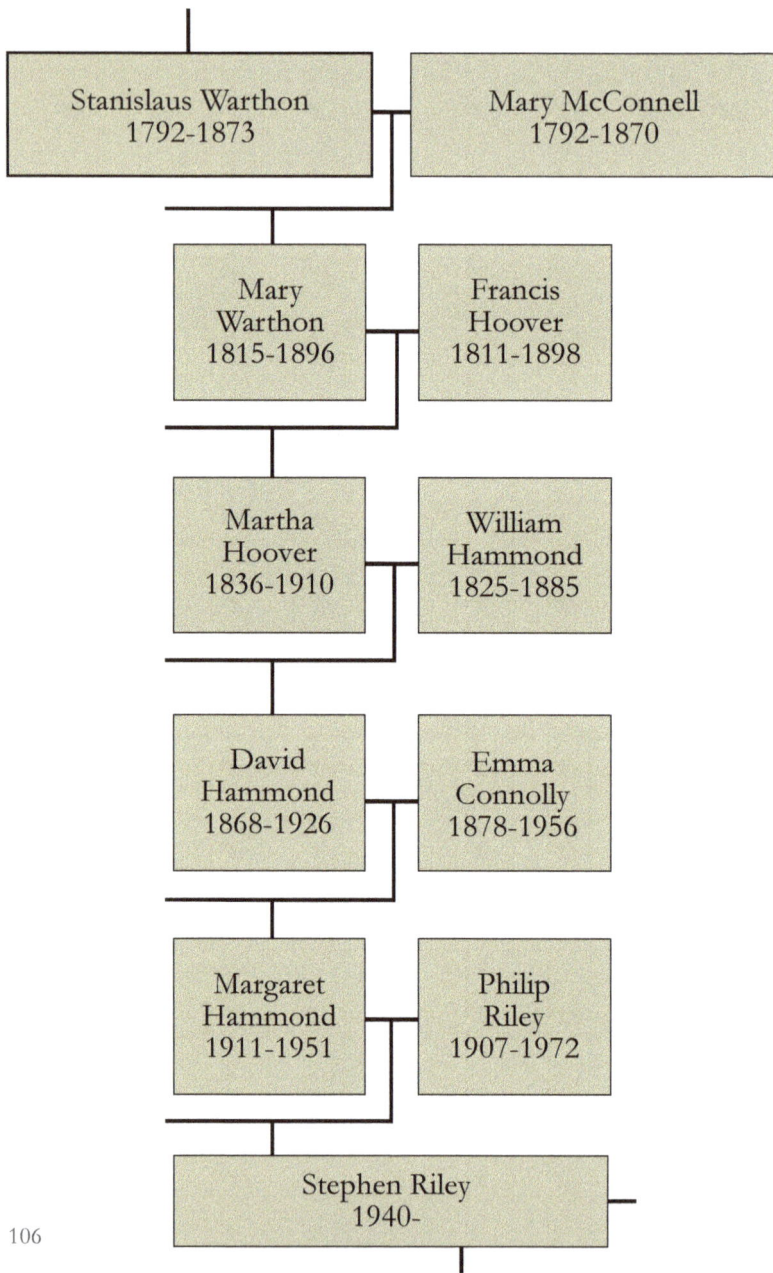

```
                    │
┌──────────────────────────┬──────────────────────────┐
│  Stanislaus Warthon       │   Mary McConnell         │
│  1792-1873                │   1792-1870              │
└──────────────────────────┴──────────────────────────┘
              │
        ┌─────────────────┬─────────────────┐
        │  Mary           │  Francis        │
        │  Warthon        │  Hoover         │
        │  1815-1896      │  1811-1898      │
        └─────────────────┴─────────────────┘
              │
        ┌─────────────────┬─────────────────┐
        │  Martha         │  William        │
        │  Hoover         │  Hammond        │
        │  1836-1910      │  1825-1885      │
        └─────────────────┴─────────────────┘
              │
        ┌─────────────────┬─────────────────┐
        │  David          │  Emma           │
        │  Hammond        │  Connolly       │
        │  1868-1926      │  1878-1956      │
        └─────────────────┴─────────────────┘
              │
        ┌─────────────────┬─────────────────┐
        │  Margaret       │  Philip         │
        │  Hammond        │  Riley          │
        │  1911-1951      │  1907-1972      │
        └─────────────────┴─────────────────┘
              │
        ┌──────────────────────────┐
        │  Stephen Riley           │
        │  1940-                   │
        └──────────────────────────┘
                    │
```

IX.

Conclusion

In conclusion, the first seven chapters presented facts about the characters in our story. Chapter VIII presented some possible theories using those facts. One hopes that readers have also come to the conclusion that Catherine the Great's daughter and our mysterious ancestor are really the same person. To recap:

NAMES

Consider the names of our characters. One has to wonder if these are just coincidences or if there's reason and choice behind them.

- Catherine the Great wanted to name her daughter Elizabeth, to honor the Empress Elizabeth, but Elizabeth insisted the girl be named Anna, after Elizabeth's sister.
- De Daschkopf's name on most records is Ann and the marriage record lists her as Ann OR Elizabeth.
- Gallitzin often referred to de Daschkopf as Catherine, which he says was her "Christian name." And of course, this is also the name of the person who might be her mother.
- De Daschkopf gave the name Stanislaus to her first and only son. Stanislaus was also the name of Anna Petrovna/ de Daschkopf's assumed father, Stanislaus Poniatowski.
- De Daschkopf named one of her children Catherine.
- De Daschkopf's last name is similar to Dashkov, the influential family connected to the Russian court and to Catherine the Great.

BIRTH DATES

The birth dates are close considering how genealogy records are known to vary.

- Catherine the Great's daughter was born at the end of the

year in December 1758.
- LDS records say de Daschkopf was born "about" 1759.
- We believe that her last name and her birth date were changed when her identity was changed and that would place her new birth date in 1759, which is consistent with the LDS records.

DECEPTIONS

In reading the biographies and autobiographies of the people involved in our story, it has been particularly fascinating to recognize the many times people have camouflaged their true identities or motives. This gives further plausibility to our theories, since they were all comfortable with frequent deceptions.

Catherine the Great:

- It seems hard to imagine that such a public figure would have so much privacy in her life, regarding her relationships with her many lovers and her resulting pregnancies. Not one of the children born to her is a child of her husband, Peter III. She kept secret her third pregnancy, by the use of loose clothing, and the excuse of an injury, and when the child was about to be born, the household was lured outdoors by the burning of a near-by home. The baby was taken away to a safe place and it wasn't until years later that his true parentage became known.
- Catherine's memoirs end, without explanation, following her frank discussion with Empress Elizabeth about the difficulties of life with husband Peter, the love she felt for Poniatowski, and the decision that she could see her children on a more regular basis. Her document ends in mid-sentence (Troyat, 119). She was about 30 then, and lived another four decades.

- Of all of the children she had, her only publicly claimed child was her first, Paul (Oldenbourg 307).
- In the late 1760s, a French writer wrote a scathing book attacking Russia, its institutions and living conditions. Since no one in France was willing to write a rebuttal, Catherine decided to write "The Antidote" anonymously. She had the first two parts published in 1771. By 1773, tiring of the writing, she told a friend the rest would never be written "because the author was killed by the Turks" (Troyat 212).

Ekaterina Dashkova:

When she traveled to Europe for the first time, she used the name Mikhailkova. By traveling incognito she avoided bringing lots of fancy clothes, or entertaining and spending lavishly. By the second and longer trip, however, she traveled less simply and frugally (Woronzoff-Dashkoff 95).

Father Demetrius Gallitzin:

He came from a well-known, wealthy noble family, yet he chose to travel to America in simple fashion, using the name Augustine Schmettau, or Smith, keeping that name for 17 years. In 1809, he admitted to his noble birth and resumed his birth name.

Ann Elizabeth de Daschkopf Warthon:

One wonders why her marriage record lists her as Ann OR Elizabeth, or why only one record says her name is Ann Knopp, and most interestingly and unusual is that there seems to be no record of the first three decades of her life. What was she trying to hide? Did she practice deception fearing that if her royal birth became known, her life would be in danger? We are told that all of the Warthon family records were passed on to de Daschkopf's grand daughter, Alice, but that they burned in a fire (Boucher vol 4, 43). Is this true? Maybe there were some revealing facts someone wanted to hide.

FRIENDSHIP AND AFFINITY

One could just say Gallitzin was a good shepherd to all members of his flock, yet there seems to be a closer affinity between him and de Daschkopf (and her family) than with others in the Loretto community.

- Catherine the Great was Gallitzin's godmother.
- Gallitzin's family served the Russian government.
- Gallitzin founded the Catholic community of Loretto in 1799, yet it wasn't until after 1809 when "Father Smith" began to be known again by his childhood name of Demetrius Augustine Gallitzin that de Daschkopf and her family journeyed to join him in Loretto, PA.
- De Daschkopf worked for Gallitzin in his household as a spinner and weaver. Her family worked for him as well.
- Few individuals are named specifically in Gallitzin's will, yet he left a considerable portion of his money to de Daschkopf and to her daughter-in-law. Some of the orphans to whom he left money were also connected to her son's in-laws.

Perhaps time will tell whether we have come to the correct conclusions about Anna Petrovna, the child born to Catherine the Great, and our ancestor, Ann Elizabeth de Daschkopf Warthon. It's been fun considering the possibilities. Now the question is, are we right?

X.

Bibliography

BOOKS AND ARTICLES:

American Philosophical Society. "The Princess and the Patriot, Ekaterina Dashkova, Benjamin Franklin, and the Age of Enlightenment," Exhibit. February 17-December 31, 2006. Philadelphia, Museum of the American Philosophical Society: 2006. Web. www.amphilsoc.org

Boucher, John and John Jordan. *A Century and a Half of Pittsburgh and Her People*, vol. 4. New York, Lewis Pub. Co.: 1908. Web. www.archive.org.

Brownson, Sarah. *Life of Demetrius Augustine Gallitzin, Prince and Priest.* New York; Cincinnati, Pustet and Co.: 1873. Web. www.archive.org.

Catholic Trails West. The Founding Catholic Families of Pennsylvania-vol.1, St. Joseph's Church, Philadelphia (1733). Eds. E. Adams and B.B. O'Keefe. Baltimore, Clearfield Company Inc., Genealogical Publishing Co. Inc.: 2004. Print.

Cronin, Vincent. *Catherine Empress of All the Russias.* New York, William Morrow and Company, Inc.: 1978. Print.

Cruse, Markus, & Hoogenboom, Hilde. *The Memoirs of Catherine the Great.* New York, Modern Library: 2006. ebook.

Dashkova, Ekaterina. *The Memoirs of Princess Dashkova.* Trans. and Ed. Kyril Fitzlyon. Intro. Jehanne Gheith. Afterward A. Woronzoff-Dashkoff. Durham and London, Duke University Press: 1995. Print.

Gallitzin, Demetrius. *The Memorandum Book and the Account Book of Rev. Demetrius A. Gallitzin, Servant of God.* Ed. Luis Escalante. Lexington, Create Space Pub.: 2016. Print.

Gallitzin, Demetrius. "Pascal Confessions and Communions, and Confirmations" at Loretto, Cambria, Co., PA., 1810-1813. Records of the American Catholic Historical Society of Philadelphia. Vol. III. Page 399-415. Web. Digital Library @Villanova University.

Heuser, Herman. "Some Forgotten Records of Prince Demetrius Gallitzin." American Catholic Historical Society. Philadelphia: date unknown. Web. Digital Library @Villanova University.

Kittell, Ferdinand. *Souvenir of Loretto Centenary. October 10, 1899: 1799-1899.* Cresson, PA, Swope Bros., Printers: 1899. Web. www.archive.org.

"Cause for the Canonization of Servant of God Demetrius Gallitzin, Apostle of the Alleghenies." Diocese of Altoona-Johnstown. Hollidaysburg: date unknown. Web. www.demetriusgallitzin.org.

Oldenbourg, Zoe. *Catherine the Great.* Trans. A. Carter. New York, Pantheon Books, Random House: 1965. Print.

Troyat, Henri. *Catherine the Great.* Trans. Joan Pinkham. New York, E. P. Dutton: 1980. (Original work published France, Librairie Flammarion, 1977). Print.

The United States and Russia- The Beginning of Relations 1765-1815. Ed. N.N. Bashkina et al. Joint Soviet-American Editorial Board. Washington, Government Printing Office: 1980. Print.

Woronzoff- Dashkoff, A. *Dashkova, A Life of Influence and Exile.* Philadelphia, American Philosophical Society: 2008. Print.

CHURCH RECORDS:

St. Augustine Catholic Church, St. Augustine, Cambria County, PA.

St. Michael's Catholic Church, Loretto, Cambria County, PA.

OTHER RECORDS:

Cambria County, PA archives
* *Stanislaus Wharton's Last Will and Testament*

Newspapers: www.newspapers.com
* Ann Warthon Obituary. Democrat and Sentinel, Ebensburg, Pennsylvania, April 8, 1857. Page 3.
* Mary Warthon Obituary. Cambria Freeman. June 2, 1870. Page 60.

Pennsylvania Wills and Probate Records, 1683-1993.
* *The Last Will and Testament of Demetrius Augustine Gallitzin, parish priest of St. Michael's Church, Loretto, PA. April 25, 1840.*

United States Census Records

ONLINE WEBSITES:

www.ancestry.com

www.familysearch.com

"Andrey Yakovlevich Dashkov." *Wikipedia, The Free Encyclopedia*, Wikimedia Foundation. 19 May 2016. Web. 10 Oct. 2016.

"Catherine the Great." *Wikipedia, The Free Encyclopedia*, Wikimedia Foundation. 9 Dec. 2016. Web. 10 Dec. 2016.

"Demetrius Augustine Gallitzin." *Wikipedia, The Free Encyclopedia*, Wikimedia Foundation. 11 July 2016. Web. 12 Aug. 2016.

"Elizabeth of Russia." *Wikipedia, The Free Encyclopedia*, Wikimedia Foundation. 6 Sept. 2016. Web. 23 Sept. 2016.

"John Carroll (bishop)." *Wikipedia, The Free Encyclopedia*, Wikimedia Foundation. 7 July 2016. Web. 12 Aug. 2016.

"List of Grand Duchesses of Russia." *Wikipedia, The Free Encyclopedia*, Wikimedia Foundation. 19 Aug. 2016. Web. 12 Oct. 2016.

"Stanislaw August Poniatowski." *Wikipedia, The Free Encyclopedia*, Wikimedia Foundation. 13 Sept. 2016. Web. 14 Sept. 2016.

"Yekaterina Vorontsova-Dashkova." *Wikipedia, The Free Encyclopedia*, Wikimedia Foundation. 12 Aug. 2016. Web. 12 Aug. 2016.